FOR SUCCESS IN ALL WE DO

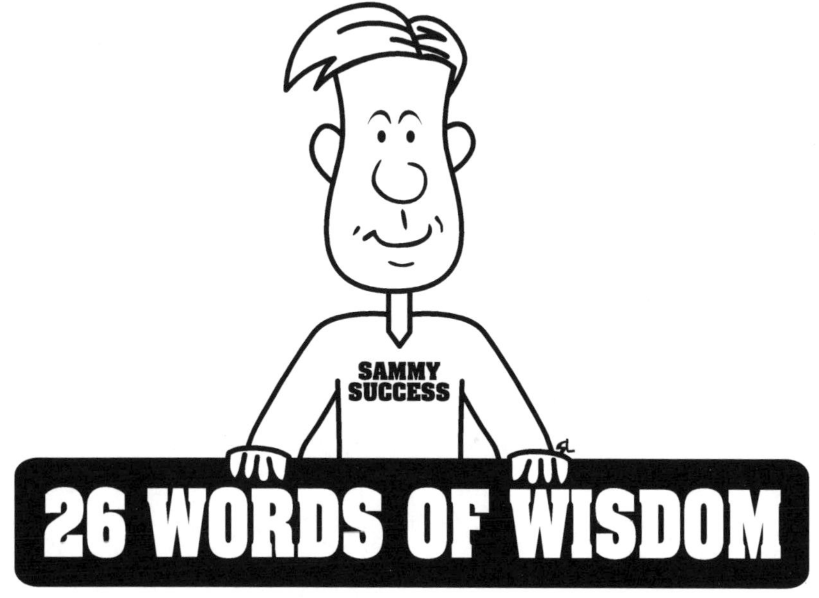

"SUCCESS TIPS FROM A TO Z"

YOUR SHORT AND SIMPLE GUIDE TO PERSONAL SUCCESS

JA Surrell, MD

JAMES A. SURRELL, M.D.

The ABC's for Success in All We Do

26 Words of Wisdom

Your Guide to Personal Success

James A. Surrell, M.D.

Cover and Illustrations: Stephanie Lake

Layout and Design: Stacey Willey

Published by

BEAN BOOKS, LLC, Newberry, Michigan

Printed by

Globe Printing, Inc., Ishpeming, Michigan

globeprinting.net

ISBN # 978-0-9825601-9-8

First Printing, January 2016

FORWARD

I have known Dr. Jim Surrell for a number of years. He is a practicing surgeon, a noted author, and also a highly respected motivational speaker. He is considered to be a national expert on nutrition, dietary weight loss and personal motivation. He has helped many people enjoy personal success by making good lifestyle choices.

I agree with the personal success recommendations reviewed in *The ABC's for Success in All We Do* book. It gives us a brief straight-forward review of proven success principles. Just these first three will certainly contribute to our personal success: A – Attitude is our choice every day, B – Believe in ourselves, and C – Choices can and will contribute to personal success.

This book also serves to remind us all that we are the ones ultimately responsible for our personal success. I encourage you to make the choice to review the brief 26 ABC concepts in this book. I truly believe they will help you on your own journey to personal success.

Tom Izzo, Head Coach
Men's Basketball
Michigan State University

The ABC's for Success in All We Do

INTRODUCTION

Each and every one of us has within ourselves the capability to become personally successful, regardless of what we choose to define as our personal success. Ultimately, we are the one who is truly responsible for our own personal success. It is so important to understand that we live by choice and not by chance. Our choices will lead to the results we obtain. We all make choices every day, and our good choices will certainly lead to good results and contribute to our personal success.

This short and simple ABC book will give you a review of time-tested and proven basic concepts that will guide you along your path to success. As we bring these ABC's into our way of thinking, this will serve as our guide to make good choices. Our important personal choices include what we choose to think about, our choice of spoken and written words, our personal actions, and how we choose to interact with others. So get started today as you choose to have a positive attitude, choose to believe in yourself, and you will indeed be on your way to personal success.

26 Words of Wisdom from A to Z

A = Attitude is our very important personal choice every day

B = Believe in yourself and be your own Best friend

C = Choices will determine our personal success

D = Discipline yourself and Deliver what you promise

E = Education is exercise for our mind

F = Faith will overcome Fear every time

G = Goals are our dreams with deadlines

H = Honesty is being true to yourself and to others

I = Imagination and visualization should be positive

J = Just keep going

K = Knowledge will come from experience

L = Listening is an art that we all must learn

M = Monitor your progress

N = Never gossip

O = Opportunities abound and are all around us

P = Persistence will always lead to success

Q = Questions are always better than assumptions

R = Respect yourself and others

S = Sleep at least seven hours per night

T = Thank You can never be said too many times

U = Utilize the skills and talents of yourself and others

V = Value your true friends, for they are priceless

W = Words are very powerful tools

X = X-out any thoughts of failure and focus on success

Y = Yesterday, Today, and Tomorrow

Z = Zip-it – Sometimes our best choice is no words at all

Your ABC Success Summary - Page 58

ATTITUDE

We have the ability to choose our attitude and this is one of the most important choices we make each and every day. We can choose to have a positive attitude or we can choose to have a negative attitude. This daily choice is very important and will significantly impact our personal interactions with family, friends, co-workers, and others. Clearly, a positive attitude will guide us toward successful actions and outcomes.

Look at the wisdom in the following profound quote from Mr. Henry Ford. "Whether you think you can, or if you think you can't, you're right." Mr. Ford certainly understood the power of the thoughts we choose as we enter into any new situation. What Mr. Ford is really telling us is that our choice of either a positive or a negative attitude will significantly impact whether we achieve positive or negative results.

William James is considered to be the father of American Psychology, and one of the first scholars to recognize the vital importance of our attitude.

> *The greatest discovery of my generation is that human beings can alter their lives by altering their attitudes of mind. - William James*

A – Attitude is our personal choice every day

T – Think positive and you will get positive results

T – Think without limits

I – Inspiration comes from within

T – Treat yourself and others with respect

U – Unlimited opportunities await your positive attitude

D – Delete all negative thoughts

E – Expect to succeed and expectations will be realized

B

BELIEVE IN YOURSELF

If you truly believe in yourself, then you already know the answer to the following question. Who should truly be your best friend? This is a very important question, and clearly, there is only one correct answer. The answer is YOU! This is a very, very important personal choice. Of course, we must always be honest with ourselves and continue to assess the results of our thoughts and actions. As we truly become our own best friend, we will learn from both the successes and the failures that we all experience in life.

We must take pride in our success, and also learn from these positive experiences in our life. We all will certainly make mistakes, and know that this is just a part of being a member of the human race. We do not need to pick on ourselves or put ourselves down. None of us can change the past. We do need to learn from both the positive and negative experiences that we all will have, and just move on.

Believe in yourself, and the rest will fall into place. Have faith in your own abilities, work hard, and there is nothing you cannot accomplish. - Brad Henry

B – Be your own best friend

E – Enthusiasm will contribute to your success

L – Listen to the thoughts and ideas of your "inner self"

I – I will be positive and positive results will follow

E – Every day will be a great opportunity for success

V – Value your family and friends

E – Expect to succeed, and know that success will come

C

CHOICES

We live by choice, not by chance. We have been given this remarkable ability to choose what we think about. In this regard, it is so very important that we choose to have positive thoughts, and choose to avoid negative thoughts. We should think of our mind as a garden, and we are the master gardener. The thoughts we choose are the seeds we plant in our garden. Therefore, as the master gardener in control of our thoughts, we should choose to plant good seeds (positive thoughts), and we will indeed get good results. We should always recall the wisdom from Mr. Earl Nightingale's classic motivational book, "The Strangest Secret". He describes this profound wisdom in just six short words: "We become what we think about."

It is important to understand that each and every one of us will become a product of the personal choices we make. Every choice we make will have consequences and, without question, our good choices will lead to our personal success. Of course, we cannot always choose what happens to us in life, but we can always choose how we respond to what happens to us in life. Ultimately, we all will become a product of our personal choices.

It is our choices that show what we truly are, far more than our abilities. - J. K. Rowling

C – Choose to have a positive attitude every day

H – Honesty is my best and only choice

O – Offer to help others in need

I – I will choose to be my own best friend

C – Choose spoken, written, and email words with care

E – Every choice we make will have consequences

S – Success will be the result of our good choices

D

DISCIPLINE

We all have jobs and tasks to do on a daily basis. Of course, we must discipline ourselves to complete these tasks and deliver what we promise. As we discipline ourselves to do what needs to be done, it is also important to assess when do I need to get this done? When you do this, you are looking at things from the standpoint of "what and when". With regard to what you may be working on, it is important to understand the wisdom of the following question: "Am I doing the right things, or am I just doing things right?"

In other words, assess what you are doing, and ask yourself if this is really what I should be doing right now, and if it will indeed contribute to your success. If it will contribute to your success, then you need to assess when does it need to be completed. With this self-discipline, we will indeed be able to deliver what we promise to ourselves and others.

Discipline is the bridge between goals and accomplishment. - Jim Rohn

D – Do today what you know should be done today

I – I will deliver what I promise

S – Self-discipline will lead to success

C – Choose to spend wisely and to save regularly

I – I will discipline myself to avoid excess debt

P – Persistence and patience will lead to success

L – Listen and learn from others you trust and respect

I – Ignore all negative comments directed toward you

N – Never, ever give up

E – Exercise both your mind and your body

EDUCATION

It has been said that education is exercise for the mind. Often without realizing it, or thinking about it, we all learn new things every day. It may have been from something said to us, or something we read, heard on the radio, saw on TV, or something new that we learned from a friend or co-worker. Education today comes from so many sources. We may learn from formal classroom teaching, from on-line computer classes, from on-the-job training, and certainly from discussions with family, friends, co-workers and others.

Of course, the internet is a valuable source of information, but we all must be careful to critically assess the sources of information on the internet. It is usually a good idea to be sure you can verify new information from more than one source. This will generally allow you to look at new information to see whether it is based on proven facts. With regard to the source of any new information, I believe it is always a very good idea to follow the wisdom contained in this wise old saying, “Consider the source.”

The great aim of education is not knowledge but action. - Herbert Spencer

E – Education is exercise for your mind

D – Direct your learning toward meeting your goals

U – Unlimited opportunities to learn are there every day

C – Continuing to learn is a life-long process

A – Ask questions and then truly listen to the answer

T – Teaching others is also a great way to teach ourselves

I – I am responsible for my learning and education

O – On-line education is a great learning resource

N – Nobody has all the answers

FAITH AND FEAR

It is generally recognized that the opposite of "Fear" is "Faith". Perhaps this is best put into perspective by the following quote: "Fear knocked on the door. Faith answered the door. There was no one there." It certainly is part of our human nature to experience fear at various times in our life. Of course, if we are faced with a serious or dangerous and potentially even life-threatening situation, then fear is our friend.

The concept of fear has been studied by psychologists for many years. It is now a well known and accepted fact that many of the fears that we generate in our mind never come to pass. When one has fear, often created in our mind, these fears will ultimately lead to worry. When we worry and are focused on something negative that "might" happen, we certainly are not focused on a successful outcome. Let us all learn from the wisdom contained in the following statement. "Do the thing you fear, and the death of fear is certain." Fear will always be overcome by faith and know that faith will always give hope to ourselves and to others.

Resist fear. Fear will never lead you to a positive end. Go for your faith and what you believe. - T. D. Jakes

F – False

E – Evidence

A – Appearing

R – Real

F – Faith

A – Always

I – Is

T – The

H – Hope

G

GOALS

Of course, we all have dreams and desires for what we want our future to be. To dream is a very good thing as we look to the future with a positive outlook and imagine what we can accomplish in the future. We should also write down our dreams for our future and focus on them from time to time as we pursue success in our life. So what is the difference between a dream and a goal?

Simply stated, a goal is a dream with a deadline. If all we do is dream about some future success in our life and do not have a time frame to turn this dream into reality, then it is quite likely that it will never happen. Therefore, we should take the simple step to establish a realistic and reasonable time frame for us to accomplish this dream. Now, we have turned our dream into a goal. With our dream now being a goal, we can focus on those tasks that need to be done within a realistic time frame to achieve our dreams.

> *What you get by achieving your goals is not as important as what you become by achieving your goals. - Zig Ziglar*

G – Goals should be our dreams, but with a deadline

O – Opportunities to succeed are all around us

A – Assess your progress regularly

L – Learn from others who have achieved similar goals

S – Success comes to those who work toward their goals

HONESTY

If someone is honest, they are said to have integrity. Integrity is defined as doing what you personally believe to be what is honest and fair to yourself and others under all circumstances. Honest people do what they believe is the right thing to do in all situations they encounter. Further, an honest person with integrity is one who always treats other people with respect and with dignity.

When a person treats others with honesty, it will always reflect positively upon the reputation of that person. The opposite is also true. If a person is dishonest, it will ultimately always be found out, and they will not have a good reputation. Therefore, be true to yourself, do what you know is the right thing to do under all circumstances and your reputation as being a truly honest individual will be a very positive part of your life. And yes, your personal reputation for being honest will certainly contribute to your personal success.

Honesty is the first chapter in the book of wisdom. - Thomas Jefferson

H – Honesty is being true to yourself and to others

O – Others will always learn if we are honest, or dishonest

N – Never lie or gossip

E – Everyone will appreciate our personal honesty

S – Say what you mean, and mean what you say

T – Truth in all your spoken and written words

Y – Your honesty should be an example for all

I

IMAGINATION AND VISUALIZATION

One of the most creative and powerful tools that we have within our mind is our imagination. Well, “imagine” that! The source for the word “imagine” comes from the word “image”, so our imagination allows us to create and visualize an image in our mind. Imagining is the ability to form new images and sensations in our mind that have not been perceived through our senses of sight, hearing, and our other senses. Our brain has this marvelous ability to create and choose these images and sensations in our mind.

Because we have the ability to choose our thoughts, we should always choose to have positive imaginations and visions in our mind. When we imagine, we are using our wonderful mental ability to form powerful mental images. Therefore, we should always visualize success and imagine ourselves being positive and successful in all we do.

If you can imagine it, you can achieve it. If you can dream it, you can become it. - William Arthur Ward

I – If I can imagine and visualize it, I can do it!

M – My visualization will always be positive

A – Always pay attention to your imagination

G – Goals will come from my positive imagination

I – I will inspire myself by mental images of my success

N – Nothing can stop me now

E – Expect to succeed and success will happen

J

JUST KEEP GOING

Know that each one of us will experience setbacks and delays along the journey to achieve our goals leading to personal success. We all will have things happen to us that we first view as setbacks. However, be aware that some of these things that happen to us along our journey are not always true setbacks. Sometimes, these so-called setbacks may steer us in a new direction and they often represent a new learning opportunity for us. When these events occur, look to see if this may be a learning opportunity and if so, learn from it, and just keep going.

Every time we decide to just keep going and not give up, we will continue to benefit from our persistence. Know that as we persist and keep going, we will stay on course to achieve our goals and we will achieve personal success.

Don't watch the clock. Do what the clock does. Keep going. - Sam Levenson

J – Just keep going one day at a time
U – Utilize your personal skills to get the job done
S – Stick with it and it will get done
T – Thank others who encourage you to keep going

K – Know that you will succeed if you just keep going
E – Every day brings opportunities to keep going
E – Expect to succeed and this will help you keep going
P – Persistence will always get the job done

G – Giving up on a worthwhile goal is not an option
O – Others are there to help us keep going
I – I will succeed because I will just keep going
N – Never give up on your worthwhile goals
G – Goals will be accomplished as you just keep going

KNOWLEDGE

It is one thing to learn the basics or even the textbook information about a specific subject, but it may be quite different to have true knowledge about that specific subject. Knowledge may be defined in various ways. Having true knowledge about something may be referred to as knowing the facts, having the correct information, or even acquiring certain skills through experience and education. Having knowledge also implies that a person has a practical understanding of that specific subject.

A person with knowledge is said to have understanding, comprehension, grasp, command, or even mastery of a specific subject. We have all heard the following term used to describe certain people who just can't wait to learn something new, because they truly have, "A thirst for knowledge". Our learning and various experiences will allow us to gain knowledge and our knowledge will lead to wisdom.

To acquire knowledge, one must study; but to acquire wisdom, one must observe. - Marilyn vos Savant

K – Knowledge will come from experience

N – Nobody has all the answers

O – Offer your knowledge to help others in need

W – Wisdom will come from knowledge

L – Learn from both positive and negative experiences

E – Experience leads to knowledge leading to wisdom

D – Don't make assumptions

G – Gain knowledge from every personal experience

E – Every day is an opportunity to gain knowledge

LISTENING

The noted brilliant author, Wilferd Peterson, gave us the term "The Art of Listening". I absolutely agree with the concept of listening truly being an art. Further, listening is an art that we all need to practice in our personal communication. We need to learn many things to be successful in our life, and I believe one of the most important communication skills we all need to learn is the art of listening.

Personal communication is a two way street of speaking and listening. When we truly listen, we will definitely contribute to successful communication in many situations we all face on a daily basis. I use the term "active listening". Active listening is a skill that is really very easy to learn and practice. When you make the choice to be an active listener, you need to stop whatever else you are doing and focus on truly listening. When we practice "active listening", we focus on what is being spoken to us. There is so much wisdom in these three words, "Listen and Learn".

I remind myself every morning that nothing I say this day will teach me anything. So if I'm going to learn, I must do it by listening. - Larry King

L – Learn and practice the “Art of Listening”

I – I will be an “Active Listener”

S – Silence is often our best choice

T – Talk only without interrupting others

E – Evaluate your listening skills frequently

N – New knowledge will come from active listening

MONITOR YOUR PROGRESS

We are often asked the following question. "How are you doing?" This is usually a sincere question that is asked by someone who cares about the person to whom the question is directed. However, there is also a very important question that we should frequently ask ourselves, "How am I doing?" This will allow us to periodically focus on how we are doing with regard to accomplishing the goals we have set for ourselves.

Certainly, if we are not quite on track toward accomplishing our personal goals, we should not pick on ourselves. We need to always remember to be our own best friend. As we take a periodic look at our goals, we can assess whether our goals and deadlines are still realistic and appropriate. If not, then we should revise and update them. Again, it is always a good idea to periodically monitor how we are doing with regard to our goals, and also very important to enjoy the ride along the way.

> *I demand pretty aggressive goal setting and a commitment to measured progress towards those goals because I don't like surprises. - Abigail Johnson*

P – Persistence will always lead to success

R – Remember to thank others who help you

O – One day at a time

G – Give yourself credit for each small step along the way

R – Review your goals with your trusted friends

E – Evaluate your progress frequently

S – Seek help when needed

S – Success will come in the proper time frame

N

NEVER GOSSIP

Gossiping is defined as an exaggeration or fabrication of a story of a personal, intimate, or private nature, regarding somebody other than the person telling the story. People who gossip almost always do so because of their low personal self-esteem. When a person gossips, they lose trust and credibility with their friends, acquaintances, co-workers, and others. Gossiping will always take away from a person's ability to achieve personal success.

It goes without saying that none of us should ever gossip. Our words are very powerful and we will often be judged by the words we use. Further, if you are in a personal conversation with someone, and you note that they are starting to gossip, then I suggest you politely make this statement. "Excuse me, but I really don't want to hear what you are saying, because this certainly is none of my business."

You will contribute to your personal success by never gossiping and by not listening to others who start to gossip when speaking to you.

Whoever gossips to you will gossip about you.
- Spanish Proverb

G – Grant yourself the choice to never gossip

O – Omit gossip and gossipers from your life

S – Stop others who want to gossip to you

S – Speak only what you know to be true

I – If you can't say something nice, don't say anything

P – People who gossip to you will also gossip about you

O

OPPORTUNITIES ABOUND

Opportunities abound and are around us all the time. It is very important to pay attention to our surroundings, to ideas that pop into our heads, to something we just saw, heard or read, and from many other sources. In fact, we all are exposed to potential ideas and opportunities for success on a frequent basis. It is therefore important to be mindful that there are numerous sources of potential opportunities for success all around us.

Consider the fact that there are many highly successful millionaires and billionaires, who truly believed that their ideas represented potential opportunities for great success. They often created opportunities, recognized additional opportunities, put their ideas to work and, as they say, the rest is history. Just a few notable examples would be Walt Disney, Bill Gates (Microsoft), Steve Jobs (Apple Computer), Mark Zuckerberg (Facebook), Howard Schultz (Starbucks), Angie Hicks (Angie's List), Tom Monaghan (Domino's Pizza), Sam Walton (Walmart), Hendrick Meijer, (Meijer Stores) and many others.

> *The pessimist sees difficulty in every opportunity. The optimist sees the opportunity in every difficulty. – Winston Churchill*

O – Observe and learn from others

P – Persistence will lead to success

P – Positive attitude opens the door to more opportunities

O – Offer to help others take advantage of opportunities

R – Recognize that your ideas represent opportunities

T – Time is our precious resource to be used wisely

U – Utilize the wisdom of others to assess opportunities

N – Now is often the best time to take action

I – Inspiration for new opportunities comes from within

T – Talk it over with family, friends, and others

Y – You need to be your own best friend

PERSISTENCE

"Nothing in the world can take the place of persistence. Talent will not; nothing is more common than unsuccessful men with talent. Genius will not; unrewarded genius is almost a proverb. Education will not; the world is full of educated derelicts. Persistence and determination alone are omnipotent."
– Calvin Coolidge, 30th President of the USA

One of the greatest demonstrations of the profound value of persistence is found in the personal history of one of the greatest Presidents in the history of the USA. Between 1832 and 1860, Abraham Lincoln ran in 10 elections, and he lost 7 of these 10 elections. Because of his unbelievable persistence, he went on to become our great 16th President of the USA.

1832 – Ran for Illinois state legislature – lost

1834 – Ran for Illinois state legislature again – won

1838 – Ran to become speaker of the state legislature – lost

1843 – Ran for United States Congress – lost

1846 – Ran for United States Congress again – won

1848 – Ran for re-election to Congress – lost

1854 – Ran for United States Senate – lost

1856 – Sought the Vice-Presidential nomination – lost

1858 – Ran for United States Senate – lost

1860 – Ran for President of the United States – won

"Patience, persistence, and perspiration make an unbeatable combination for success," - Napoleon Hill

P – Prioritize your goals
E – Enthusiasm is key
R – Review your progress
S – Study what others have done
I – I will persist and I will succeed
S – Seek help when needed
T – Teamwork will lead to success
E – Eliminate obstacles by facing them head-on
N – Never give up and you will achieve personal success
C – Confidence will grow with each small step
E – Enjoy the ride along the way

Q

QUESTIONS ARE ALWAYS BETTER THAN ASSUMPTIONS

How many times have we all made this rather humbling comment? “Well, I thought you meant...” We usually wind up making a comment like this after we realize that what we “assumed” about a specific situation was not really anywhere close to what was really going on with that situation. In other words, when we learned about something that we had to do, but we weren’t quite sure of the details, we made assumptions.

Of course, what we really should have done is to merely ask a few simple questions, and everything would have been clearly understood. So, how do we avoid these potentially embarrassing situations in the future? Let’s not make this complicated. Here is my short and simple recommendation regarding this matter. “What is the only bad question? It’s the one you don’t ask.”

The art and science of asking questions is the source of all knowledge. - Thomas Berger

Q – Questions not asked will never be answered

U – Understanding comes from actively listening

E – Express your understanding by repeating the answer

S – Seek answers from other people you respect

T – There is no such thing as a bad question

I – If not perfectly clear, ask questions

O – Okay to honestly reply, "I don't know."

N – Never make assumptions, and always ask questions

S – Successful learning comes from asking questions

RESPECT YOURSELF AND OTHERS

Having self-respect is clearly associated with being our own best friend and it will have a significant impact on our personal success. Our respect for others shows the other person that we truly care about their feelings and for their well-being. Further, we treat other people with respect not only by what we may say to them or act toward them face to face, but also what we may say about them to others when they are not around.

Having self-respect also means that a person has pride and confidence in themselves. Numerous studies have proven that those who have this self-respect are less prone to blame, guilt, regret, and stress.

Respect your efforts, respect yourself. Self-respect leads to self-discipline. When you have both firmly under your belt, that's real power. - Clint Eastwood

R – Recognize the efforts of others

E – Every person is truly special

S – Speak only the truth

P – Praising others shows them respect

E – Earn self-respect by your personal positive choices

C – Choose to offer positive words to those you respect

T – "Thank You" can never be said too many times

S

SLEEP AT LEAST SEVEN HOURS

Numerous scientific studies have proven that adults need a minimum of seven hours of sleep every night. Seven hours of sleep is necessary to allow both our immune system and our nervous system to function properly. Too little sleep will leave us drowsy, unable to concentrate, and will also impair our memory. This will, of course, have a negative impact on nearly all our daily activities.

It has been proven time and time again that adults who get at least seven hours of sleep each night feel more energetic and alert. They also experience less illness because this allows our immune system to repair and rebuild itself during these seven hours of rest. The result is that our immune system is much more effective in fighting off both minor and major illnesses. Getting the recommended minimum of seven hours of sleep per night is very important and will most certainly impact our overall health and personal success.

Sleep is that golden chain that ties health and our bodies together. - Thomas Dekker

S – Seven hours of sleep a day leads to your good health

L – Let your body rest to stay healthy

E – Energize your immune system with 7 hours of sleep

E – Energy and alertness comes with 7 hours of sleep

P – Personal health increases with 7 hours of sleep

T

THANK YOU CAN NEVER BE SAID TOO MANY TIMES

The words "thank you" show your gratitude and appreciation to others. These two very special words should be used as a sincere recognition of some goodness or kindness that we have received. Your verbal statement or a written thank you note will be truly appreciated.

In today's fast paced internet society, we sometimes send or receive "thank you" notes in the form of an email or a text message. There are times when this may be appropriate, but if we are really thanking an individual for their kindness, an email or text message likely will not carry the same positive impact as a hand written note, phone call, or personal face to face "thank you".

Of course, when we receive a verbal "thank you", it is important to politely respond with a sincere "you're welcome". When we respond with "you're welcome", we let the other person know that we also appreciate their "thank you".

There's not a day that goes by when I don't get up and say thank you to somebody. - Rod Stewart

T – "Thank You" can never be said too many times

H – Helping others is a great way to show thanks

A – Always thank others who help you

N – Never forget to reply, "You're Welcome"

K – Know your true friends and thank them often

Y – Your "Thank You" words and notes are appreciated

O – Opportunity to show you care for kindness received

U – Use your words often to thank others

UTILIZE THE SKILLS AND TALENTS OF YOURSELF AND OTHERS

In the same fashion that no one person has all the answers, none of us truly has all the skills and talent to accomplish all that we need to do to achieve our personal success. It is extremely important that we truly assess our own personal skills and various talents. We should then use our own skills to accomplish those things for which we have genuine talent.

For those other areas where we may not have certain skills, we should then use the specific skills of other people, including family, friends, co-workers, and others. By working together in this manner, we will now be able to complete those tasks that will help lead to our personal success. Further, working with others may also offer us a great opportunity to learn new skills and develop new talents that will serve us very well on the path to our personal success.

You cannot add more minutes to the day, but you can utilize each one to the fullest. - Menachem Mendel Schneerson

U – Use your time wisely

T – Thank others for sharing their skills

I – I will share my skills and talents

L – Learning new skills will lead to personal success

I – I will deliver what I promise

Z – Zest for learning will lead to new talents

E – Education will lead to new skills

V – VALUE YOUR PRICELESS TRUE FRIENDS

True friends are those individuals who remain available to help each other. A true friend is one who is never too quick to judge our thoughts, words, or actions. A true friend is one who is willing to listen to you. A true friend is one who will never lie to you, never gossip about you, and will come to your support when you are in need of friendship. Further, a true friend is someone who will give you the freedom to be yourself.

A true friend is one who is always there to help. A true friend will not tolerate others saying untrue and negative things about you. Your true friends will not force themselves on you, but they will be quick to ask if they can be of help to you if they believe you need some help. And yes, without question, your true friends will absolutely contribute to your personal success.

A true friend never gets in your way unless you happen to be going down. – Arnold H. Glasow

V – Value true friends

A – Appreciate others

L – Listen and learn

U – Unite with friends

E – Everyone has value

F – Friendship is contagious

R – Respect others

I – I will be my own best friend

E – Evaluate yourself first

N – Never lie or gossip

D – Do not be too quick to judge

S – Share a positive attitude

WORDS ARE VERY POWERFUL TOOLS

"Words are very powerful tools – use them, don't abuse them." Our words have the power to have a strong positive or negative influence, so we need to choose our words wisely.

It is wise to understand that our spoken or written words may well be passed on to others. Today, our email words may often find their way to many places not intended. Therefore, it is wise to be very careful with the written words we choose to send out in our emails.

It is a well known fact of life that we all do what is called "self-talk". Without really thinking about it, we all probably engage in self-talk each and every day. Because we have the ability to choose our thoughts, it is the best choice to choose positive self-talk, and choose to avoid any negative words said to ourselves.

There is much wisdom about words in the following quote.

If you wouldn't write it down and sign it, then don't say it. – Earl Wilson

W – Welcome

O – Others with

R – Respect, with

D – Dignity, and with

S – Sincerity

X-OUT ANY THOUGHTS OF FAILURE AND FOCUS ON SUCCESS

Everyday we should choose to have a positive attitude, to believe in ourself and to be our own best friend. It is also very important to always recall that we live by choice, and not by chance. We have this marvelous ability to choose our thoughts, so we need to focus on thoughts of success and not on thoughts of failure.

One of the most profound works ever written about our personal thoughts is the classic book by Earl Nightingale, "The Strangest Secret". Here is what Mr. Nightingale defines as "The Strangest Secret". *We become what we think about!* Further, he explains to us that the thoughts we choose and the various things we think about will always come to pass. Yes, we will indeed become what we think about.

Once you replace negative thoughts with positive ones, you'll start having positive results. - Willie Nelson

S – Success will come to those who focus on success

U – Understand that we will become what we think about

C – Choose to have a positive attitude

C – Choose positive thoughts about personal success

E – Expect to succeed

S – Seek help from others when needed

S – Serve others who need your help

YESTERDAY, TODAY, AND TOMORROW

There is much wisdom in the following quote. "Yesterday is gone, forget it; tomorrow never comes; today is here, use it." This tells us that today is really the only time we have to accomplish anything. There are so many times when we should just follow the advice in these three motivational words. "Do it now."

Every day we have been given the opportunity to choose our thoughts and to choose our actions. It is so important to be positive everyday and to always be your own best friend. We all need to understand that every day is a gift and we need to focus daily on what is important to us.

It is also important take some time to relax and enjoy the gift of today.

Yesterday's the past, tomorrow's the future, but today is a gift. That's why it's called the present. - Bill Keane

T – Take some time to relax each day

O – One day at a time is profound advice

D – Don't put off what you know should be done today

A – All of us have 24 hours to be used wisely every day

Y – Yesterday is gone, learn from it, then forget it

Z

ZIP IT – SOMETIMES OUR BEST CHOICE IS TO USE NO WORDS AT ALL

How many times have we all made a comment or a statement that we wish we never would have made. Of course, we all have done this. It is certainly is in our best interest and will contribute to our personal success if we truly think before we speak. It may even be a statement made in response to a question asked of us. Know that it is always OK to respond with this comment, "You know, that is a great question, and I really want to think about that before I answer." It is also OK to reply to a question, "I don't know."

This "Zip It" choice also fits in with the concept of the "Art of Listening". When we are in a conversation with others, it is important that we truly listen. Remember that our conversations are two-way streets and we need to give others the opportunity to respond to our questions. We also need to take note of how others are listening to us.

One of the most sincere forms of respect is actually listening to what another has to say. - Bryant McGill

S – Silence is golden and is often our best choice

I – I learn from my listening, and not from my talking

L – Learn and practice the "Art of Listening"

E – Engage others by actively listening to what they say

N – No words at all from me may well be my best choice

C – Choose to listen and learn from others

E – Every successful person is a good listener

Your ABC Success Summary

From my personal experience and that of so many others, major contributions to our personal success will come from making it your choice to follow the time tested advice contained in just the first three letters – ABC. Of course, you now know these to be:

A – Attitude is our personal choice every day

B – Believe in yourself and be your own Best friend

C – Choices will determine our personal success

If we choose to have a positive attitude every day, and choose to be our own best friend, our ability to make choices leading to our personal success will naturally follow. In this regard, I must say that it is usually a rather profound and significant learning experience for all of us when we truly understand that we all live by choice, and not by chance. Therefore, many of the decisions that we all make every day represent our personal choices. As we make the good choices that contribute to our success, this will reinforce our being our own best friend, and will also contribute to our positive attitude.

Without a doubt, one of the most important choices that we make all day long is that we choose what we think about. I believe that the greatest early writing on this concept was by Earl Nightingale, in his truly ground-breaking book, *The Strangest Secret*. When first published in 1956, this work was described as one of the greatest motivational books of all time. Mr. Nightingale refers to "The Strangest Secret" in just six short words: "We become what we think about."

Again, as noted in this wisdom from Earl Nightingale, it is so very important to understand that we all will eventually and ultimately become what we think about. Simply stated, if we think about success, we will become successful. Because we can truly choose what we think about, it is very important that we choose to have positive thoughts of success. Yes, as has been proven over many decades, we will indeed become what we think about. Therefore, it is essential that we never forget that we live by choice. As we choose a positive attitude and positive thoughts, leading to positive actions, we will indeed become our own best friend as we continue to enjoy and appreciate our personal success.

Make the choice to use the thoughts and ideas from these short and simple "26 Words of Wisdom" and they will indeed help you along your way to personal success. It is very appropriate that the letter "A" is the first letter of the alphabet. This first letter should also serve to remind us all that one of our first choices each day should be our positive Attitude for that day. Never forget that we all live by choice, and not by chance. Make the choice to believe in yourself, and to be your own best friend. This positive choice will also assist us all greatly as we all travel along our journey to achieve our goals leading to our personal success.

SAMMY
SUCCESS

To Your Personal Success

I believe that we could define personal success as the progressive realization of a worthwhile goal that a person has defined as something they truly wish to accomplish. The following is a very profound quote from Celestine Chua regarding the role of our personal attitude with regard to becoming successful. "Success is 99 percent attitude and 1 percent aptitude." Here are some of my attitude thoughts in the following short poem.

ATTITUDE POEM – *James A. Surrell, M.D.*

The attitude we choose becomes our inner voice,
Our success will depend on this very key choice.

So I changed my attitude and I did nothing else,
And I chose to be positive and believe in myself.

These thoughts were uplifting within my own mind,
So I shared them with others and chose to be kind.

We all have the power to be positive each day,
And the rewards we receive we can never repay.

We all need to be careful with the words that we say,
And know that for certain, they will come back some day.

This is a great truth that we all must believe,
That which we give out, we surely will receive.

I sincerely wish you all the best on you your personal success journey. Keep your positive attitude, be your own best friend, and know that your good choices will lead to your personal success.

About Your ABC Author

Your author, Dr. Jim Surrell, has a very special interest in helping people achieve personal success. He gives frequent public and professional presentations and is a very entertaining and much sought-after speaker. He blends a significant amount of humor into his many talks. In addition to speaking about his short and simple ideas to help us all achieve personal success, Dr. Jim give numerous presentations about healthy lifestyle choices, including nutrition and weight loss, cancer screening and prevention, and other healthy lifestyle topics. He also does numerous TV appearances and also writes a very popular newspaper column entitled: "Talk With the Doc".

Dr. Jim is a highly successful board-certified colorectal surgeon and holds fellowship status in both the American Society of Colon and Rectal Surgeons and the American College of Surgeons. In addition to his best selling SOS (Stop Only Sugar) Diet book, Dr. Surrell has also authored many articles in various medical journals. He is a nationally recognized nutrition and dietary weight loss expert.

Prior to making the choice to go to medical school, Dr. Surrell had a highly successful career with the IBM Corporation. He did achieve significant personal success at IBM and was awarded the coveted IBM Golden Circle Award. This Golden Circle Award is presented annually to the top 5% of IBM marketing personnel in the United States.

Dr. Jim is committed to helping people achieve personal success and here are two of his favorite success quotes.

Success is a state of mind. If you want success, start thinking of yourself as a success. - Joyce Brothers

The only place success comes before work is in the dictionary. - Vince Lombardi

You are now
on your way to
personal success!
SAMMY
SUCCESS
SL

Made in the USA
San Bernardino, CA
26 April 2016